Lightning Bolt Books™

How Drones Work

Anna Leigh

Lerner Publications ◆ Minneapolis

Lerner Publications Company
A division of Lerner Publishing Group, Inc.
241 First Avenue North
Minneapolis, MN 55401 USA

For reading levels and more information, look up this title at www.lernerbooks.com.

Library of Congress Cataloging-in-Publication Data

Names: Leigh, Anna, author.
Title: How drones work / Anna Leigh.
Description: Minneapolis : Lerner Publications, [2019] | Series: Lightning bolt books. military machines | Includes bibliographical references and index. | Audience: Age 6-9. | Audience: Grades K to 3.
Identifiers: LCCN 2018043338 (print) | LCCN 2018043860 (ebook) | ISBN 9781541557420 (eb pdf) | ISBN 9781541557413 (lb : alk. paper)
Subjects: LCSH: Drone aircraft—Juvenile literature.
Classification: LCC TL685.35 (ebook) | LCC TL685.35 .L45 2019 (print) | DDC 629.133/39—dc23

LC record available at https://lccn.loc.gov/2018043338

Manufactured in the United States of America
1-46152-45951-12/11/2018

Table of Contents

What Is a Drone?

A small aircraft flies across the sky. No pilot is on board. This aircraft is a drone.

Drones fly using remote controls. A pilot on the ground flies the drone. These pilots can stay in one place and fly drones in different countries!

The military often uses drones. **Some of them take pictures.** Others may make maps or help with rescue missions.

Maps help guide the military in unfamiliar places.

Drones fly in places that would be too dangerous for humans. Fewer people have to go into war zones thanks to drones.

The History of Drones

The US military has wanted to make planes without pilots for years. It first tried to create drones in the early twentieth century. These drones were never used in battle.

The military began using drones in the Vietnam War (1957–1975). These drones took photos and helped the military gain information.

The Ryan Firebee was one of the first drones to see military action.

Other countries soon began using drones for military work. They made drones that could fly farther and for a longer time.

Some new drones fly without remote controls. An operator gives the drones instructions before they take off. Then the drones follow the instructions on their own.

Parts of a Drone

Most drones have wings, a propeller, an engine, and fuel. The engine of a large military drone is similar to the engine used in a snowmobile.

Drones are made of light materials. This helps them move quickly and fly long distances.

The camera shows the pilot where the drone is going.

Drones also have sensors. These include cameras, night vision cameras, and radar systems. These sensors help pilots control the drone.

Some drones carry weapons. Lasers or GPS help these weapons reach their targets.

Drones at Work

Drones come in many different sizes. Some are as small as a bug. They fly for only a few minutes at a time.

Other drones are large and powerful. Their wings can be as long as 130 feet (40 m) across! They may fly for forty hours or more.

The RQ-4 Global Hawk can fly up to 60,000 feet (18,288 m) above the ground.

The military is making new drones. They will have better cameras and controls so they will work even better.

The US military is working on new drones that travel on the ground and in water.

One day, more drones might be able to complete missions without a human controller. Military drones will continue keeping people safe.

Drone Diagram

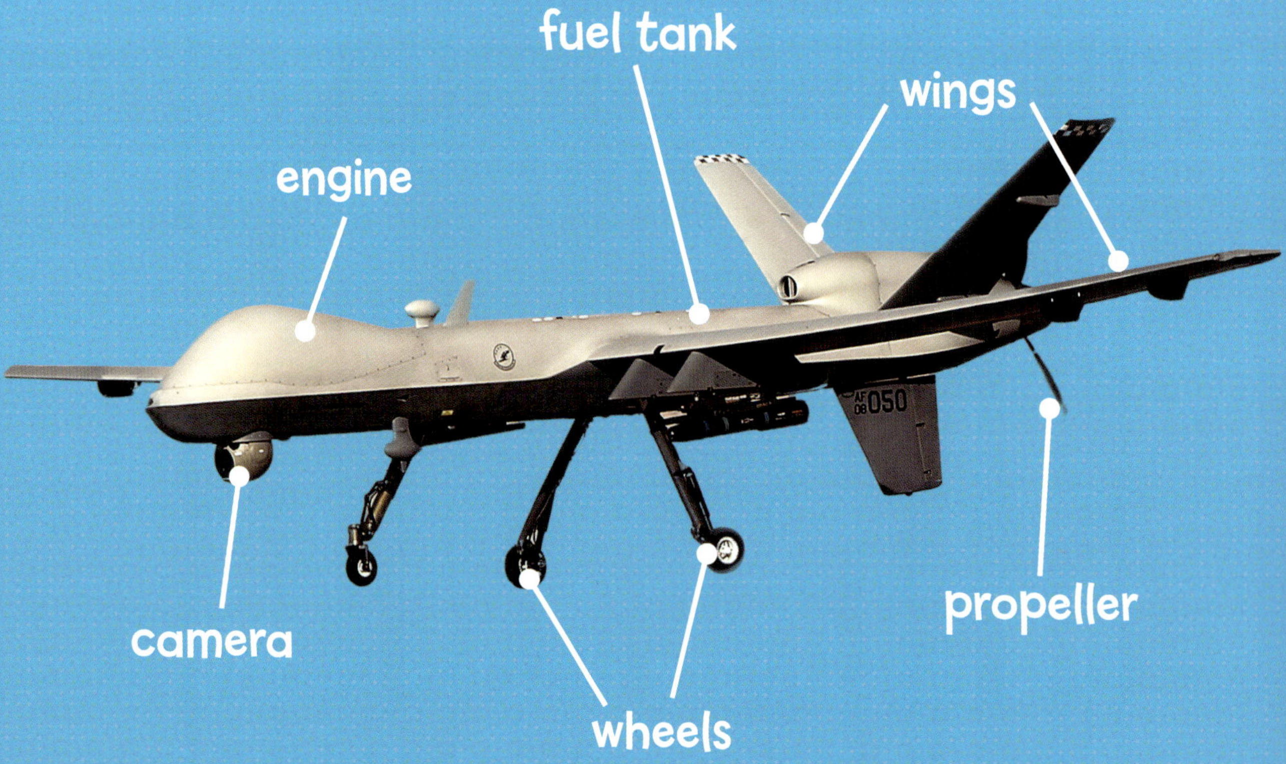

Drone Facts

- Drones are named after male bees. Early drones made a buzzing sound, but modern drones are very quiet.
- About ninety countries use military drones. Only eleven of these countries have drones that carry weapons.
- Between 2001 and 2016, more than four hundred US military drones crashed. It sometimes costs more than $2 million to repair the damaged aircraft.

Glossary

engine: a machine that uses fuel to power moving objects

GPS: a system that uses satellites to determine an exact location

laser: a very powerful beam of light

pilot: a person who flies an aircraft

propeller: a set of blades that spin quickly to help a vehicle move

radar: a device that helps aircraft detect objects using radio waves

sensor: a device that detects and responds to heat, light, sound, or movement

target: an object to shoot at or attack

Further Reading

About the Army: Aircraft, Helicopters, and UAV
https://www.goarmy.com/about/army-vehicles-and-equipment/army-helicopters-and-uavs.html

Boothroyd, Jennifer. *Inside the US Air Force*. Minneapolis: Lerner Publications, 2018.

Facts about Drones
http://mocomi.com/drones/

Larson, Kirsten W. *Drones*. Mankato, MN: Amicus High Interest, 2018.

Mangor, Jodie. *Drones*. Vero Beach, FL: Rourke Educational Media, 2016.

Military Aircraft for Kids
http://bambo-jambo.com/military-equipment/military-aircraft-for-kids

Index

Photo Acknowledgments

Image credits: US Army, p. 2; US Navy, p. 4; US Army photo by Sgt. Samuel Northrup, 7th Mobile Public Affairs Detachment, p. 5; US Air Force photo by Jamal Wilson, p. 6; US Army photo by Sgt. Russell Gilchrest, p. 7; US Air Force, pp. 8, 15; National Museum of the US Navy/Flickr, p. 9; GEORGES GOBET/AFP/Getty Images, p. 10; US Marine Corps photo by Cpl. Ashley E. Beckett, p. 11; US Army photo by Cpl. William Howard, p. 12; US Marine Corps, p. 13; Ethan Miller/Getty Images, p. 14; US Marine Corps photo by Lance Cpl. Austin Mealy, p. 16; US Air Force photo by Tech. Sgt. Frank Miller, p. 17; John Joyce/Naval Surface Warfare Center, p. 18; US Navy photo by Mass Communication Specialist 2nd Class Ryan D. McLearnon, p. 19; Isaac Brekken/Getty Images, p. 20; US Marine Corps photo by Cpl. Jodson B. Graves, p. 23.

Cover: US Air Force photo by Bobbi Zapka.

Main body text set in Billy Infant regular 28/36. Typeface provided by SparkType.